SEX-LOVE

in

CHRISTIAN MARRIAGE

First Published in 1973 by the Australian Catholic Truth Society.

Republished in 2009, 2023 by Connor Court Publishing Pty Ltd
with the new introduction by Fr Anthony Percy

Copyright of the 2009 edition © Anthony Percy

Connor Court Publishing Pty Ltd
PO BOX 7257
REDLAND BAY, QLD 4165

www.connorcourt.com
sales@connorcourt.com

ISBN: 9781922815439

Cover photo taken from iStockphoto

Printed in Australia

SEX-LOVE

in

CHRISTIAN MARRIAGE

With an Introduction by

Anthony Percy

CONNOR COURT PUBLISHING

TABLE OF CONTENTS

Introduction

The booklet, Sex Love In Christian Marriage, was initially published by A.C.T.S Publications, Melbourne. The author is unknown. The original publication simply said, "By C.M.S."

Despite the author's anonymous status, the booklet went through no less than thirteen printings. I came across it just after I was ordained in 1990. A woman working with the Billings Family Life Centre, Young, NSW, introduced me to it.

It is an interesting and important booklet. It deals with sex. More precisely it deals with the "science" of sex. That is, how best to do sex.

The booklet was written in 1973. The layout and language of the booklet indicates this, but much of the material is perennial.

The booklet has four brief chapters. The first two deal with "Love-making." Chapter three deals with the orgasm and chapter four looks at questions that may arise as people prepare, engage and reflect on sex.

I asked for permission to write a new introduction to the booklet. The Billings Group gladly granted it. From 1979 to 1984, Pope John Paul II taught the Theology of the Body. George Weigel described the Theology of the Body as a theological time bomb. Many authors have tried to detonate the "bomb." My book, *Theology of the Body Made Simple*, may be helpful.

The Theology of the Body is magnificent. We live in a time of great confusion with respect to sex. It was not so long ago that people felt constrained in talking about sex. Today, sex is the topic. We have gone so far in our advertising as to think that cars are sexy. We have gone from one extreme to another.

The Theology of the Body and indeed Sex Love In Christian Marriage lie between these polarities. Sex-love, according to John Paul II, is that act that unites a man and woman in love. Through this experience of sex-love, the couple come back to themselves, so to speak, with a renewed sense of their own personal identity. Furthermore, when they unite physically in the act of sex and thus form a one-flesh union, man and woman become an image of God par excellence. It is upon this union that the gift of fertility "descends" – to use John Paul's language.

Sex is important. It is pleasurable and powerful – or so it should be. It is human and it is holy – or so it should be. But often enough, it is not these realities. Often people feel used, lonely, frustrated and unholy after sex.

That is why this booklet is important. It is, in some ways, an old-fashioned booklet. It was probably designed to guide young couples on their wedding night and subsequent nights. Many of them would have been virgins upon entering marriage.

Virgins are still in existence, but the number is declining these days. That is a shame. But the booklet is still very relevant. For despite the proliferation of sex and the growth of sexual perversions in our society, many people are deeply dissatisfied with their sex lives. That is a shame, too. Sex is supposed to serve the friendship and love between husband and wife. So the booklet is valuable.

Like almost all things in life, there is a science to sex. The sex drive in men and women is strong. God designed it so. But men and women are quite different in their sexual arousal and responses. If they don't study these realities; if they don't honour these realities during sex; if they don't reflect upon these realities with each other after sex, then sex is likely to be a disaster. Husbands and wives will be like ships passing in the night. They may have some sense that someone is there, but they really won't see, feel or acknowledge each other. In other words, their intimate love won't grow.

Since the time of St. Augustine, the Church has understood that upon entering marriage, couples receive three specific gifts from Christ. Those three gifts or goods are fidelity, sacrament and children.

While this booklet does not mention these realities, it is not hard to see that sex-love plays an important role in each of them. Husband and wife share a unique friendship and fidelity – sex love serves this beautiful reality. Sex love seals the bond they have entered into on their wedding day. That bond is a one-flesh union through the words of commitment they speak and through sexual intercourse. The bond is sacramental. It is full of grace. It is from sex love, too, that new life – children – arises. Children are, accordingly to the Church, the "supreme gift of marriage."

It is the 21st Century and the Church is calling for a new evangelisation – in fact has been calling for it for some years. Many people have not heard the good news of Christ. Quite a few have forgotten it and need a reminder. Sex Love In Christian Marriage will help spread the message of Christ.

There is an old Latin phrase that applies aptly to sex: *Corruptio Optimi Pessima*. That is, the corruption of the best is worst. Sex is good. Sex is beautiful. But when it is dislodged from the intimate love of man and woman in marriage we can expect trouble. We see these difficulties widespread today.

It is hoped that this slightly new edition

of Sex Love In Christian Marriage will bring about a great change in peoples sexual lives. For sex serves marriage. Marriage serves family. Family serves society. Much is at stake.

Father Anthony Percy

April 2009

INTRODUCTION
TO THE ORIGINAL EDITION[1]

These notes are intended as a guide to the practice 'of sex-love' for married couples. Their aim is strictly practical, but, at the same time, they are meant to be read in the context of the whole Christian view of marriage as a way of Christ like life, a way of loving God and becoming holy. You cannot, in fact, separate the theological and moral principles of Christian marriage from its actual practice. Any so-called "sex technique" which is not based on the fact that sex-love is the expression of love

---

[1] What follows is the original introduction. I have made only a few slight alterations. One corrects a misprint in the text and the other corrects a minor or mild theological misunderstanding.

between two persons who have been given by God the vocation of sanctifying each other, is not only bad theology and bad morals but also bad 'technique"; it simply does not work well.

Unfortunately, most of the books available on the practice of sex-love are written by non-Christians and, even when their advice does not go against Christian morals - contraception is usually taken for granted and masturbation sometimes recommended - they often reduce the act of love to a set of mere physical tricks. It is not surprising that Christian married couples are often worried when they read these books and wonder how far they can follow their advice.

On the other hand. Christian writers on the subject tend to go to the opposite extreme. They admit, of course, that sex-love is good in itself and an essential part of marriage, but they tend to suggest that if husband and wife have the right spiritual attitude towards marriage the sexual side will more or less look after itself. Unfortunately, it is a matter of bitter experience that the sexual side of marriage does not look after itself. The number of cases of real unhappiness in marriage caused by misunderstandings about sex-love, even where husband and wife are of completely good will, shows that very clearly. But, even when these misunderstandings do not create unhappiness, couples who take sex-love for granted, so to speak, miss a great deal of the richness of married life; their marriage is not as perfect as it might be.

Sex-love is not something extra or incidental to marriage but it is rather the normal means by which husband and wife express their love. For this reason, the expression of their married love – the sex-act – should be done as perfectly as possible. When it is done well and worthily it brings about very deep and intense happiness between husband and wife, not only physical satisfaction but a happiness of the whole person. And, in turn, this happiness between them has a direct influence on the personal formation of their children. The proper performance of sex-love, then, is important for the mutual love between the partners, but also for the responsible procreation and personal formation of the children. In practice, it is not possible to dissociate the two.

It is, then, precisely because it is infinitely more than a purely physical gesture that sex-love is not just an automatic business, like eating and sleeping, which more or less looks after itself. It is because it is bound up with the whole person that it has to be learned, that one has to be educated gradually in its ways and means. And this learning is a delicate and subtle and never-ending process calling for the utmost understanding and consideration from both partners. (Ideally husband and wife educate each other in sex-love.)

What we have tried to do here is to give as

simple and yet as complete a guide as possible to the practice of sex-love, concentrating especially on those questions which seem most often to cause difficulties to newly-married couples. We have avoided long physiological and anatomical descriptions because they usually only confuse the average reader and besides, give the impression that advice about sex-love is a "medical" business, which could not be farther from the truth. These observations are necessarily very general and may appear sometimes over-obvious; each couple must apply them to its own case. The descriptions, too, may seem at times rather "mechanical", but that is inevitable in matters like this where precise detail is all important. Unless advice on sex-love is quite specific it is quite useless.

That raises the question whether it is right to speak publicly about these matters at all. It is not, of course, a matter of moral principle which is at issue because, as we have said, sex-love is good in itself and it is therefore good to speak about it. But things good in themselves may be put to wrong uses and everyone knows that detailed descriptions of the act of sex-love, such as are contained in this book, may be read by the immature and taken up in the wrong way. That possibility must honestly be taken into account when we decide to publish a book of this kind. However, it seems to us that the good this little book might do for married couples far outweighs the possibility of it being put to a wrong use.

1

LOVE-MAKING:
THE PART OF THE HUSBAND

First, we must define the terms which will be used in this book. It is amazing how many people are unable to ask for specific advice about matters of sex-love because they simply do not know the terms to describe the various sex-organs and functions; they suffer from a complete lack of vocabulary. The act of sex-love is called by various names: "sexual intercourse", "the sexual act", "sexual relations", "sexual union", "the marital act" , "the conjugal act".

The act takes place when the male sex-organ the "penis" becomes "erect", that is to say, rigid and elongated through sexual stimulation, and is inserted into the female sex-organ or "vagina", the long sheath-like opening in the woman's body which has its entrance in the cleft between her thighs. The "vagina" leads to the "uterus" or "womb" where the baby is formed when "conception" takes place. After the "penis" has been inserted into the "vagina", a kind of nervous spasm called the "orgasm" or "climax" or "ejaculation" or "emission" takes place in the male sex-organ so that it ejaculates or emits into the "vagina" a thick transparent fluid, the "semen" or "seed" or "sperm". The "semen" carries the male cells, "spermatozoa" or "sperms", which are capable of fertilising the female cell or "ovum" contained in the woman's "fallopian tubes". When this fertilisation takes place this is called "conception" and the woman is said to have "conceived". Of course not every act of sexual intercourse causes "conception". When the act of sex-love is properly performed an intense nervous reaction similar to the male "orgasm", or "climax" or "satisfaction", also takes place in the female sex-organs.

The Act of Sex-Love

We can now go ahead and give a detailed description of an act of sex-love. But we must emphasise again that it is only intended as a general outline and that it is based upon "the average couple", who of course, do not exist. Each couple must work out their own way of love-making by trial and error.

The basis of the whole procedure of sex-love is simply this: because it is the expression of the love of one person for another person, successful sex-love requires perfect harmony between mind, body and emotions in both partners.

It is an act of the whole person and the preparatory "lovemaking" must aim at making each partner ready to engage and offer the whole of himself or herself in the act of love. But this harmony between mind, body and emotions comes about in quite different ways for men as compared with women. A man is physically ready for intercourse in a matter of seconds, but it takes some time and some preparation before he is mentally and emotionally ready. With the woman it is quite different. Her body usually responds much more slowly and gradually and, this is the important point, only after she is in love mentally and emotionally. With the woman it is mind and emotions first and body second. With the man it is body first and mind and emotions last. It is this difference of sexual make-up between husband and wife which makes preparation for the act of sex-love absolutely necessary. This preparation or love-making is a real art in which both partners have a complementary and indispensable part to play in bringing each other to that state of complete harmony of mind, body and emotions necessary for successful sex-love.

The Beginning

It is usual for the husband to begin the act of sex-love, although it is good for the wife to learn to take the initiative. At any rate, in the first phase of love-making it is the husband who plays the main part. The woman, we just said, becomes physically ready for intercourse only when she is brought into a state of deep mental and emotional love for her husband. The task of the husband then is primarily to bring his wife into this state of mental and emotional love. The difficulty here, however, is that many men, having read the usual cheap sex-books, or heard the crude and misleading sex-talk of other men, imagine that the woman can be made ready for intercourse simply by physical stimulation, by touching, kissing, and caressing her breasts or sex-organs for example. No doubt she can often be aroused in a very superficial way by these means, but, more often than not, it will probably prevent her from achieving her orgasm when actual intercourse takes place. The woman who has been prematurely stimulated in this physical way exclusively, feels ready for intercourse and then when union occurs she suddenly loses desire and interest and often finds it difficult to achieve her orgasm. Even when she does have a superficial kind of orgasm she will often feel unsatisfied and disappointed after it. This is because she has been stimulated too quickly with the result that her whole mental and emotional attitude is out of tune with her physical state. Her body is aroused but her mind and emotions remain completely cold, so that her whole response is, so to speak, dislocated. Physical stimulation has, of course, a very important part to play in love-making, but in its proper place.

The husband's main concern in this first

phase of love-making should be to work upon his wife's mind and emotions. He must show his love and affection for her, speaking to her affectionately, telling her how much he loves her, recalling intimate experiences together, kissing her and embracing her lovingly. Whatever physical stimulation is attempted at this stage should be gentle and affectionate; the husband can fondle and kiss his wife's breasts, for example, or gently touch and stroke her thighs and sex parts, the entrance to the vagina, for instance, and the "clitoris" at the top of the vaginal cleft. Many men, of course, feel that "love-talk" is not in their line and they feel some embarrassment in using endearments. However, just as the woman has to overcome her natural shyness in love-play, so the husband has also to learn to overcome his embarrassment at having to declare his affection openly to his wife.

Without trying to generalise about the famous "feminine temperament", it is true that most women look for direct and open declarations of love from their husbands. They know very well that their husbands love them but they want to be told so. A man will reason out for himself that his wife loves him from the fact that she shares his trials and cares for him, but a woman needs to be told directly. That just seems to be a fact of feminine psychology and the husband must recognise and respect it.

This preparatory phase may take up to a quarter of an hour or even more. Some women, of course, react more quickly than others and the same woman may react differently on different occasions. The only rule that can be given is that this phase of love-making should continue till the woman is aroused to a state of deep love for her husband so that she then desires to take an active part in the love-making herself.

A point by the way here. When it is obvious that both partners desire sex-love then it is a good idea to discard clothes, pyjamas, etc., from the beginning. In any case they should be discarded at the end of this first phase of love-making. The husband might help his wife to undress. To try to have intercourse wearing pyjamas or nightdress is an unnecessary hindrance to the freedom and intimacy of the act of sex-love.

Showing Affection

We have just been speaking of the need for the husband to show his affection for his wife in love-making, but it is important also for the husband to realise that his wife looks for these declarations of affection and loving attentions outside actual sex-love itself. Many women feel that their husbands are only interested in them when they want to engage in sex-love and they feel that they are being used simply as an instrument of their husband's selfishness.

It is quite proper for husband and wife to engage in love-play, for the husband to fondle his wife's breasts or sex-parts, caressing and kissing, for example - outside actual intercourse, provided of course that neither is brought to the stage of having an orgasm separately. The only rule, if one can so put it, for love-play is that neither party should have an orgasm outside the act by which the semen or seed is emitted from the male penis into the vagina. A couple may then engage in love-play without any intention of going on to perform an act of sex-love, though sometimes, if carried on too long, this can be a physical and nervous strain, especially for the husband. Continual sexual excitement without culminating satisfaction in an act of sex-love can be dangerous to some extent in that it may lead to difficulty in achieving the "orgasm" or "climax" in intercourse.

In general, however, as we have said, this kind of love-play has an important part to play in marriage, above all in the case of newly-married couples where the wife often needs to be prepared gradually in this way to become more confident in love-making so that she too may play her proper part in the act of love.

2

LOVE-MAKING:
THE PART OF THE WIFE

We said before that the husband is physically ready for intercourse in a matter of seconds. His sex-organ, the penis, becomes erect so that it can penetrate into the vagina and he can bring about his orgasm. That being the case, he may imagine that he is completely ready and requires no special preparation for the act of sex-love. But that is a great mistake. If he engages straightaway in intercourse he will experience that curious sense of frustration and disappointment which so many men feel after the act of sex-love. This is, in fact, caused by the same kind of disharmony between his mental and emotional attitude on the one hand and his physical state on the other which, as we saw in the case of the woman, prevents the achievement of the act of sex-love in all its richness and intensity.

It is the task of the wife then to bring about this harmony in her husband so that he, in turn, can give himself wholly to her. In the first phase of love-making it was the husband who was the main actor: but now in this second phase it is the wife who takes the initiative. If she has been aroused to a state of deep love she will naturally use the beauty and charms of her body, giving her breasts to her husband etc., to arouse the love of her husband in turn. From now on it is she who dictates the course of love-making and the husband remains almost passive, at least physically, in a state of deep affection and love for his wife, filled with happiness and a sense of security in her response. It is important that the husband should encourage his wife to take an active part in lovemaking for it is essentially a business where each has a specific and indispensable part to play; the couple has literally to "make" love, to bring it into being by their own mutual art.

A Difficulty

It is usually very difficult for women to be perfectly free, at first in love-making and to realise that they have an active part to play. That of course is quite natural in newly-married wives.

Often, however, one finds women, married for a long time even, who think that to be too interested in sex-love or to play an active part in it is "un-lady-like" or "immodest". They are prepared to engage in sex-love for the sake of their husbands but they regard it as an ordeal to be gone through.

"Modesty" in Marriage

This raises the whole question of "modesty" in marriage and we will digress for the moment to consider it. Before they were married, husband and wife were modest in a way proper to them as single people. They were aware of the sacredness of their bodies and especially of their sexual functions and so took care of their bodily behaviour, dress, etc., in a way proper to single people. But when they were married they began to share in a common vocation; they became one in a sense, so that everything which applied to them individually before now applied to them together. Thus there is a modesty proper to them now as a married couple, a common or mutual modesty, an awareness and care of the sacredness of their union together in the face of outsiders. But within that union they should regard and treat each other's bodies with absolute freedom and intimacy: they are "two in one flesh". Thus it is altogether normal and desirable that husband and wife dress and undress together and bathe together for instance; in general, to be perfectly free with each other's bodies. There is, so to speak, no modesty between them; there is only a modesty about their union together with respect to other people. They should always be aware of the sacredness of that union and never betray it. One sometimes finds couples who think it amusing to joke with others about their sex-relationships together. That shows an appalling lack of respect for their married modesty and leads inevitably to a cheapening of their whole marriage.

Of course, as we said before, it is not easy for women especially to unlearn the modesty proper to their former single state and to learn this new kind of married modesty. When you have lived singly for twenty or thirty years you cannot learn this new way of living in common overnight. Husband and wife must help to educate each other and especially in the first year of marriage, must show a great deal of understanding towards each other. In cases, and there are many, where the wife has to overcome a real repugnance to sex-love, the husband must help her to learn confidence so that she gradually takes her proper part in love-making and learns to see and use sex-love as an essential part of her married life.

"Bad Thoughts"

The question of so-called "bad thoughts" is also connected with this question of modesty and something can be said about it here. By "bad thoughts" or "impure thoughts" is meant usually thoughts about sex-love. In fact, however, there is no such thing as a "bad thought" in itself, for the act of sex-love is good in itself and therefore good to think about. It is the circumstances alone which make it good or bad to think about acts of sex-love. Thus, for a single man to think in detail about acts of sex-love may be "bad" because it may lead him to sin by deliberate sexual pleasure and masturbation. In other circumstances however, if he is preparing to get married for instance, not to think of acts of sex-love and take a rational pleasure in his thoughts would be bad. Again, for a married man to think about acts of sex-love with someone not his wife is evil because it is a betrayal of fidelity to his wife. But for a married man to think with pleasure of acts of sex-love with his wife, where such thoughts do not lead to masturbation, is quite normal and in no sense evil.

It is a very good idea in fact for husband and wife to get into the habit of thanking God in their prayers for the happiness they have found in acts of sex-love with each other. As with all good things, God should be thanked for particular occasions of sex-love. This helps, moreover, in forming a positive and open attitude towards sex-love in both husband and wife.

The Second Phase

To return now to our description of the second phase of love-making. Because, in this phase, the wife uses the beauty of her body to captivate and charm her husband, it is a good idea that the lights be left on. This may seem a little strange and embarrassing at first, but it does help a great deal to make both partners completely free with each other. At times the couple will just relax in embrace at other times their love-making may be quite vigorous and playful. Love-making should never be solemn or dull but a happy and free-and-easy business. Above all, husband and wife must learn to speak quite openly to each other during love-making; the husband for instance should not just guess that his wife is ready, he should ask her.

This second phase of love-making ends when the wife is so aroused, so deeply and completely in love that if she continued love-play any longer she would have her orgasm. This phase may take anything from fifteen to thirty minutes and it is impossible to give a set time for this whole preparation. Sometimes the husband may find it difficult not to have his orgasm before his wife is ready. This is usually due to too much concentration on his physical state. If he concentrates upon his wife during this second phase he should have no difficulty in retaining his orgasm until his wife is ready.

3

THE ORGASM OR CLIMAX

The preparation for the act of sex-love ends when husband and wife are completely one, in mind, body and emotions, in their desire for union. They can now offer themselves as whole persons to each other. This offering culminates in the orgasm or climax by which the husband's sex-organ, the penis, discharges the semen or seed into the vagina. The husband's orgasm often brings about his wife's orgasm at the same time or a little after so that both are one in this beautiful act of love.

Sometimes the wife's orgasm begins before that of her husband, sometimes after.

It goes without saying that for the husband to withdraw his penis prematurely and to have his orgasm separately, is against the whole meaning of sexual intercourse. "Withdrawal" - an old and primitive means of contraception - also usually has severe psychological effects particularly upon the wife.

Physical Changes

Before we go on to describe this orgasm or climax however, it will be as well to consider the mutual physical changes which have been taking place meanwhile in both husband and wife. In the husband, as we have said, his sex-organ, the penis becomes longer and quite rigid or "erected" and usually remains in that state during the period of love-play. In addition a cleansing fluid prepares the channel in the penis for the flowing of the semen and there is no cause for worry if it should flow from the penis during love-play. As for the wife, first of all the exterior of her sex-organs becomes firmer and the clitoris, a small projection towards the top of the cleft at the entrance to the vagina, usually becomes erect and very sensitive to gentle touching, though in some women the clitoris is difficult to locate. The breasts also become firmer and the nipples may become erect and very sensitive to the touch. Most importantly the entrance to the vagina becomes relaxed and lubricated by a fluid similar to the fluid which cleanses the male penis. This fluid has nothing to do with the women's orgasm and it sometimes flows quite freely from the vagina during love-play. It is only when the vagina is relaxed and lubricated in this way that the penis can be inserted without difficulty or pain for the woman and it is of considerable importance that intercourse should not be attempted before the woman's vagina is in this state. If it is not properly lubricated, the insertion of the penis will cause her pain and most probably prevent her from having her orgasm. With a newly married woman it may make her afraid of having future acts of intercourse. Usually this relaxation and lubrication of the vagina happens automatically during the period of love-play, but sometimes a woman may find difficulty even when fully aroused and ready for intercourse. It may be advisable then to apply some oil or other artificial lubricant to the opening of the vagina to aid the insertion of the penis.

The First Intercourse

When a woman is having her first act of intercourse her hymen has to be "perforated" or broken before the penis can penetrate into the vagina. The hymen is the skin or membrane which usually covers the entrance of the vagina of the unmarried woman and its perforation during the first act of intercourse may cause some pain and result in a little bleeding. Care should be taken by the husband to make the operation as painless as possible for his wife. For this it is usually best if the wife lies on top of her husband so that she can regulate the entry of the penis into her vagina. If the hymen is too thick to be broken by the pressure of the penis or by the fingers the advice of a doctor should be sought. There is a popular superstition about the hymen being a sign of the woman's virginity and some husbands become needlessly worried and suspicious when they find in the first act of intercourse that the wife's hymen has already ,been broken. However, the hymen may often be broken quite accidentally by a woman falling or straining herself, or in the course of a medical inspection for instance, and of course this in no way signifies that the woman is not a virgin.

When the vagina is relaxed and lubricated the penis can be inserted gently into it. It is usually best if the wife guides the penis herself because she can tell then when she is comfortable. The penis should enter quite easily and without undue forcing or strain so that almost its whole length is sheathed by the vagina. Both husband and wife are then ready to have their orgasms.

Position of Partners

One other point must be discussed before we describe the orgasm itself, and that concerns the best position for successful intercourse. Generally speaking, of course, any position is appropriate and "natural" provided that it allows the depositing of the semen in the vagina. As for practical rules, the only consideration is that both partners should be perfectly comfortable and able to achieve their orgasms without difficulty. First, the bed should be quite flat and firm because it is impossible to have intercourse properly where the bed is sagging and does not give firm support. Then, as we have just said, both partners must be perfectly at their ease: we have already mentioned that pyjamas and other clothes are a hindrance and should be discarded. As for the actual positions of the partners, there is in fact no one position which is absolutely the best; what is successful for one couple is not so for another. In any case, it is good to change positions from time to time; love-play and intercourse should never become stereotyped. The most usual position is that where the husband reclines full length upon his wife who draws her thighs apart so that her husband can lie between them. In this position the penis fits easily into the vagina without any strain. To give the wife a feeling of perfect security and at the same time to make the vagina hold the penis firmly, she can draw up her legs into a flexed position and link them round her husband. He can support most of his weight on his elbows and if the woman is lying completely flat without a pillow beneath her head she will not feel uncomfortable with her husband's weight. Some women need a low pillow under their back or buttocks to help them to get into the right position, but that is a matter for experimentation.

Another common position is the exact reverse of this: that is to say the wife reclines astride her husband who lies perfectly flat. This is a helpful position when the wife needs to move about to achieve her orgasm and it also aids the husband to help her more easily by fondling her breasts, stroking her thighs, etc. It is a good position too for the wife who needs to learn confidence in love-making because she feels in a more "dominant" position. Again, where the wife is pregnant it may be more comfortable to have intercourse in this position.

Another position is where the couple lie side by side and this again may be more comfortable for the woman when she is pregnant. In this position, however, it is easy to come apart and the consequent feeling of insecurity may distract the wife and so prevent her from achieving her orgasm. A slightly more complicated position is where the partners adopt a sitting position face to face with the woman kneeling astride the man. This usually has some strain however and for most couples is not a position which can be used continually.

The Orgasm

It is difficult to describe an orgasm or climax to a person who has never experienced one. However, it is so intense an experience and so unlike any other that one can say that a person who is doubtful whether he has had an orgasm most probably has not had one. One can describe the orgasm in very general terms as a kind of nervous spasm or reaction of the sex-organs. When it is perfectly achieved however, it affects the whole body with an amazingly intense feeling of pleasurable excitement and with a wonderful sense of relaxation and peace when it is finished. The actual orgasm may occur for a minute or more and is usually accompanied by excited movements by both partners. After the orgasm is completed the penis loses its rigidity and shrinks back to its normal size so that the husband is not physically capable of another act of intercourse for some time.

Difficulties

There is usually no great difficulty for the husband to have his orgasm. If there is he should try moving his penis gently up and down in the vagina; the tip of the penis is the most sensitive part and if this is moved against the vagina it will usually bring about the orgasm. In most cases, however, the woman's movement in bringing about her own orgasm and the slight contractions of her vagina when she begins her orgasm will bring about her husband's orgasm. If the husband should find that erection of the penis is difficult for him or that he continually fails to achieve his orgasm he should consult a doctor or psychiatrist or marriage counsellor as soon as possible. It is nothing to be ashamed of, and if advice is sought early it can usually be remedied.

The woman often finds it much more difficult to achieve her orgasm, especially in the first few months of marriage. There are even cases of women who have been having frequent intercourse for two or three years, or longer, without ever succeeding in having an orgasm. There is no need to emphasize how unnatural such a state of affairs is and what bad effects it can have on the happiness between husband and wife. For the woman the act of sex-love becomes an ordeal and it ceases to be a means by which she and her husband express their love for each other. It must be emphasized then that the wife should normally, if not in every act of sex-love, achieve an orgasm. She should not think that having an orgasm is something exceptional or extraordinary and that perhaps she is the sort of woman who just doesn't have orgasms.

A newly-married wife, of course, may take three or four months, before she becomes used to love-making and ready to have an orgasm and at this stage the missing of her orgasm may not have any untoward effects on her; she may even get quite a lot of pleasure from acts of sex-love. However, if she continues like this, she may find it increasingly difficult to achieve an orgasm and this in turn is likely to have a bad effect on her.

If a woman is aroused and then cannot fully relieve the sexual tension she usually experiences a feeling of intense frustration, and if this continues over a long period it can lead to a serious nervous state. If then, after six months of married life, the wife has not succeeded in having an orgasm the advice of a marriage counsellor or a doctor should be sought. Usually, however, it is due to lack of proper preparation and can be rectified by attention to the points we have outlined here.

A Problem

Again, even with the most experienced couples the wife may sometimes miss having her orgasm, either through sickness, or tiredness, or worry, or lack of interest, causing her to lose concentration during intercourse. Most often, though, this is due to insufficient preparation. The husband may not have spent enough time in the preliminary love-making or may have attempted direct physical stimulation before his wife was mentally and emotionally ready. Or he may have neglected to allow his wife to play her full part in intercourse and to decide when actual union should take place. Whatever the cause, if the wife does miss having her orgasm after being fully aroused it can have, as we just said, a nerve-racking effect on her. At these times her husband should be especially considerate to her and by affectionate behaviour try to make up for her disappointment and frustration. If he has had his orgasm she may try to bring about her orgasm separately by using her fingers to stimulate her sex-organs, and the husband may use his fingers in the same way to help her, even after they have separated.

The perfect state of affairs is where husband and wife have their orgasms together. Sometimes they will occur together almost as soon as actual union takes place; at other times husband and wife may need to move about a little before their orgasms occur. The husband can help his wife particularly by fondling and kissing her breasts and by stroking her thighs. When it happens that he has had his orgasm before his wife he should of course remain united until she arrives at her orgasm. After he has had his orgasm the man feels relaxed and tends to lose interest, so that it takes an effort of consideration on his part to remain united and keep on helping his wife.

After both partners have had their orgasms they should remain united for some time. This is especially important for the wife who often experiences an intense "afterglow" following intercourse. They can turn on their side and remain embraced in that position. One should never finish an act of sex-love with a selfish "that's that" attitude.

It may happen sometimes after the orgasm that a little fluid flows out of the woman's vagina, but there is no need to worry about it. It will probably be mostly lubricating fluid and perhaps a little of the semen emitted into the vagina by the husband.

This, then, is the consummation of the act of sex-love, and at this moment husband and wife are really and truly "two in one flesh".

4

OTHER QUESTIONS

In this last chapter we will discuss several questions concerning sex-love which often seem to worry newly-married couples and which could not conveniently be treated in the preceding chapters.

The "Marriage Debt?"

First of all, the question of the "rights" and "duties" of husband and wife with regard to sex-love: the "marriage debt" as it is sometimes called, after St. Paul. What is the position if one partner wishes to engage in sex-love and the other, for some reason, does not? Can the one partner demand that the other allow him or her to have intercourse, much as one can exact the fulfilment of a contract or the payment of a debt? This way of looking at the matter scarcely harmonises with the Christian ideal of marriage as the sacramental union of two persons, and in fact it derives from a rather crude interpretation of St. Paul's observations on marriage.

No doubt unless there is a very good excuse, sickness for example, neither party should refuse to engage in sex-love if the other wishes to; but it is not so much a question of paying a "debt" as recognising that the other partner is offering his love and that to refuse to engage in sex-love is to refuse to accept that offering of his love. It is as though a person refused to accept a gift offered to them. Each, then, should always look upon the other's desire for sex-love not as a selfish demand for the "gratification" of his "passions", a demand for the payment of a "debt", but rather, as we have just said, as the offering of the gift of his love. And each, no matter what his or her feelings at the moment, should try, if possible, to accept that offering and try to offer himself in return as completely as possible.

Proper Consideration

On the other hand, husband and wife must exercise proper consideration for one another and when it is obvious that one or the other would find it difficult to engage in sex-love, his or her feelings should be respected. The husband, for example should realise that there are times when his wife may feel completely dry and passionless or, at other times, that she may suffer from a peculiar feeling of irritability and of not wanting to be touched, a state fairly common to some women. Again, during the time of her monthly menstrual period or in the first months of pregnancy she sometimes feels unwell and finds it difficult to have intercourse. In any case, it is essential that husband and wife speak quite openly about these things to each other so as to prevent misunderstandings. It is remarkable how many couples never discuss such questions or anything about their acts of sex-love together at all. One sometimes meets men who have been married for two or three years who do not know whether or not their wives achieve an orgasm in intercourse - simply because they have never asked them!

Frequency of Intercourse

Another question which often bothers newly-married couples concerns the frequency of sexual intercourse. How often should a couple engage in acts of sex-love? First of all it should be made quite clear that there is no kind of moral or "natural" limit to the frequency of intercourse. A couple, for example.

who engage in acts of sex-love seven times a week are not being "excessive" or acting improperly in any way; if they desire intercourse with each other as often as that, it is proper for them to have intercourse as often as that. On the other hand, solely from the physical point of view, it is often said that too frequent intercourse physically exhausts the partners, particularly the husband. There is some truth in this no doubt but, like many other ideas about sex-love, it is rather exaggerated. In actual fact, one of the main effects of sex-love is precisely the relaxing and energising effect it has on both husband and wife. Sex-love can have a completely rejuvenating effect on the wife who is tired out by the constant demand of caring for her family. Then again, a wife who sees that her husband is worried or depressed may use her charms and make love to him to help him relax his nervous tension. At any rate, it seems that the average frequency of intercourse, after the first few months of married life, is about two or three times a week. That is only an average of course and is not meant in any way as a rule. Sometimes a couple may perform acts of sex-love more frequently than that -- they may even engage in two or three separate acts together in the one night -- sometimes they will not feel the desire for sex-love for two or three weeks at a time.

Another common idea is that frequent intercourse tends to dull the mind, by concentrating too much attention on physical pleasures, and that people doing intellectual work should limit the frequency of intercourse. This idea seems to be based on a very crude conception of sex-love, as though it were merely a means of physical pleasure or "sexual gratification" completely divorced from our rational nature, instead of being seen as an act of the whole person, a means by which one person expresses love for another person. Then again, as we have just remarked, far from being a distraction to those engaged in intellectual work, sex-love may, through its relaxing influence actually be a considerable help to them.

A Matter of Adjustment

It happens sometimes that young married men after the first few months of married life lose a great deal of nervous tension (no doubt largely sexual in origin) which was the basis of their energy and drive. And this in turn seems to affect their whole outlook: they no longer feel interested in the ideals, religious ideals particularly, which inspired them when they were single and sometimes they tend to become cynical and half-hearted. Even perhaps the intense love they feel for their wives before they were married becomes colder and they feel irritated by the demands their wives make upon them.

One often meets young married men like

this who are bewildered by the change which has suddenly come over them. What they have to realise, however, is that they are leading a quite new kind of physical existence and they have to learn to adjust themselves to it. Obviously the man who is engaging in frequent acts of intercourse will be in a different physical and psychological state to a man who leads a celibate life and he must adapt himself to this state.

Positive Thinking

No doubt it is possible to lay too much emphasis on the part of sex-love in marriage. Sex-love, after all, is the means of married love and not its end. And precisely because the mysterious power of sex is so strong an element in our make-up, it can be made into an end in itself. Then it is no longer the means by which husband and wife express their love for each other but an instrument by which they use each other for their own selfish pleasure. However, the dangers of placing too much emphasis on sex-love are usually exaggerated and, in actual fact as we have said before, those who abuse sex-love in this way find that it gives them very little real pleasure.

Selfishness in sex-love, to put it at its lowest, simply does not pay. In any case one finds that where it is carried out in its full richness and intensity sex-love finds its own proper place, so to speak, in the married life of the couple and there is no need for them to worry about placing too much emphasis on it. Usually the difficulty for Christian couples is exactly the opposite, learning to see sex-love as a positive and essential part of their married life.

Time for sex-love

When is the right time for engaging in sex-love? There is, of course, no right or wrong time as such; the time is dictated completely by the desires of the couple. That the right time when the couple retires for the night is usually chosen is solely a matter of convenience and there is no reason why they should not have intercourse during the day if they want to and it is sufficiently convenient and private. It is, of course, best if husband and wife are not over-tired, though that is usually more important for the wife. Tiredness, however, can be over-emphasised for, as we said before, sex-love itself, to a large extent, overcomes tiredness and weariness and nervous strain.

A husband or a wife who continually uses the excuse of being too tired to engage in sex-love should ask himself or herself if that is the real reason. The wife who finds that she is really exhausted at the end of the day after caring for her family should try to prepare herself by resting for some time during the day so that she will be able to respond sexually to her husband. That, of course, is very difficult for a mother of a large family to do, but on the other hand she has to realise what a frustrating effect her lack of interest and responsiveness can have on her husband's love.

Should intercourse be attempted during the time of the woman's monthly "period" or "menstruation"; the discharge of blood and other matter from the vagina which occurs every twenty to thirty days and which lasts for five or so days? Once again, there is nothing improper in any way in having intercourse at this time. But the woman often feels unwell during menstruation and her vagina may feel painful so that she is not likely to desire intercourse or, if she does, to achieve her orgasm. Nevertheless, some women have their greatest desire for intercourse precisely at this time and there are cases where the woman has achieved her orgasm only by having intercourse during the menstrual period. If the husband should feel any repugnance at having intercourse at this time it might be a good idea for him to help his wife to bathe before the act of sex-love. In any case the woman's feelings and wishes should be the sole guide here - it being understood that she accepts her menstrual flow as completely "clean" and natural.

Intercourse during Pregnancy

The same applies to intercourse during pregnancy. During the first two or three months of pregnancy the woman usually suffers from "morning sickness" and feels generally unwell. Here, as before, the husband should respect his wife's feelings and allow her, during this time, to take the initiative in sex-love.

Till what time can intercourse be carried

on when the wife is pregnant? This is largely a matter for medical advice and the doctor, whom the wife is attending for prenatal care should be consulted if there is anything abnormal in her condition, especially if she has had previous miscarriages. However, the usual advice given is that intercourse can be performed up till the sixth month of pregnancy or even later without danger to the child in the womb, though of course the couple will have to be much more careful and gentle in their love-making than before.

There is no direct relation between a woman having an orgasm and conceiving a child. A woman who has never had an orgasm may conceive perfectly well. However, in cases where conception has not taken place after a long period of intercourse, the woman's having an orgasm often does seem to aid conception.

A Last Word

In all difficulties relating to sex-love the most important thing is that husband and wife should talk openly and honestly to each other.

As we said before, husband and wife have to educate each other in sex-love, and no books or external advice can take the place of that process of mutual education.

A NUPTIAL PRAYER

Tobias said to Sarah ... "You and I must pray and petition our Lord to win his grace and his protection."
She stood up and they began praying for protection.
"You are blessed, O God of our fathers;
blessed, too, is your name
for ever and ever.
Let the heavens bless you and all things you have made
for evermore.
It was you who created Adam, you who created Eve
his wife
to be his help and support;
and from these two the human race was born.
It was you who said,
'It is not good that man should be alone; let us make
him a helpmate like himself.'
And so I do not take my sister
for any lustful motive;
I do it in singleness of heart.
Be kind enough to have pity on her and on me and
bring us to old age together."
And together they said, Amen, Amen, and lay down for
the night.

(Book of Tobias. 8: 4-8; Jerusalem Bible).

www.ingramcontent.com/pod-product-compliance
Lightning Source LLC
Chambersburg PA
CBHW060741100426
42742CB00031B/2581